Tapestries of Tarot

ISBN: 9798397056946

TAPESTRIES OF TAROT

Table of Contents

The Beginning 6
The Fool 11
The Lovers 14
The Sun 24
Ace of Cups 30
Death 33
The Star 39
The Magician 42
The Hermit 45
The Wheel of Fortune 50
Temperance 55
Ace of Wands 59
The Emperor 62
Judgement 70
The Hierophant 80
Ace of Pentacles 85
The Tower 89
The Empress 94
The Chariot 97

Ace of Swords 108
The High Priestess 111
The World 116
About the Author 131

The Beginning

For those with a creative and fertile imagination, it is easy to become captivated, mesmerised even, by the imagery, lineage and legend surrounding the famed Tarot. Magical, mysterious, steeped in tales of folklore, and permeated with tendrils of occult power. Personally, I own five decks: the Rider Waite (which provides the pictorial content in this book), the Tarot of the Witches, the Luciferian Tarot, the Thoth Tarot and the Hermetic Tarot. Everyone has their own favourites of course, and there are a multitude to choose from.

To write a poetry collection centred around the Tarot's Major Arcana cards has long been a seed of a project for me. Even before that, in the black-and-white certainty and clarity of purpose of my youth, owning a bass guitar and obsessed with the goal of technically gifted virtuoso musicianship, the already immortal Tarot was to be newly re-immortalised as a double album of music. Some were to be instrumental masterpieces, mottled and interwoven with others that would sport vocal dazzle, and lyrical expertise, embedded in progressive metal showmanship. Two of my friends and I managed to craft a small cluster of adventurous, voiceless pieces in a West Country neighbourhood drawing room; The Fool, The Tower, and then something that was perplexing to attribute to a card - and was eventually christened 'Easter Island' instead.

The most obvious approach would be the simplest. A poem about each individual card, sequenced in numerical order. That is what I initially planned, but this is the Tarot, which is surrounded by intuitive forces, and so it wasn't long before I found myself veering off; selecting the subjects more instinctively, feeling my way, tuning in to the magnetism I felt for each one. The drive to go with esoteric flow and form, vibe and feeling, rather than mathematical sequence, was futile to oppose.

I had decided early on that rather than include only the Major Arcana, there should be pieces for the Aces of the four suits: Cups, Pentacles, Swords and Wands. Even then there were strong energies pulling me in directions that I had not foreseen. Inspiration had been there immediately, I found that the heritage and power of the imagery lent themselves freely to wild ideas and fluent language. But from the myriad affinities pushing and pulling and invading the narratives, it was clear that I had no need to think about these procedural questions, because the answers were going to come by themselves.

For a poet, writer, artist or musician, as many readers will understand fully, it is exhilarating when the creation snatches control from the creator and provides unseen energy and direction to the art form. It can be a very rare thing, though I have been blessed in this way many more times than I can even hope to recall. I offer my gratitude for this to the blood and genes of my ancestors, the core of spirituality within nature, the Goddess and the God, the Earth and the elements, the Universe and Spirit. The all-pervading cosmic consciousness that we are all so fortunate to be component parts of.

Once my hand and my mind opened to this controlling, inspirational energy, things formed themselves. Accordingly, the poems wrote themselves in their own order. The choices made *for me* and not *by me.* What also came to pass was that the final collection does not, in fact, contain a poem for every card, there are omissions in addition to the changes in sequential order. Whether those left out will surface and manifest themselves at some point in the future, I shall just have to wait and see.

As for the poems themselves, most, in similar fashion, flowed equally organically; the first drafts had a great deal of spontaneity to them, with relatively few exceptions. I am not quite blessed to the degree that every first take of a piece needs no editing! On occasion that is true, but usually they need a review (after a healthy period of incubation). That could be days, weeks, months or sometimes even years. Hard work and practice, as with any skill or process, trims down the frequency of mistakes, though often the accidents work out as lovely permanent inclusions as we all know.

The most sublime beauty of the Tarot is in the extrapolations, and existential expansions, of interpreting the cards. The order in which they are drawn. Whether they are upright or inverted. Where the cards are, relative to each other, and, most importantly, the question posed for the reading. In writing these poems, as is clear on reading them, any and every angle enters the frame. From superficial face value to deep message, to schizophrenic tangent or development.

It seems I am fast becoming known as 'The Schizophrenic Poet' which serves to inform people, before diving into reading my works, of the oddity of styles and nature of expression they might expect to encounter. I have written about the illness in earlier books and have more such material to come; I am not at all afraid to broadcast the matter. Yet the more well-known I and my projects get, the less need there is for the reader to have to 'understand' the pieces in a conventional sense.

So! To the matter in hand. Join me on an astroscopic journey of the astral wonders of the timeless Tarot. Expressed through abstract contexts, divinations and, sometimes, literally, 'mad' vocabulary and syntax. I hope you enjoy the quest.

Stuart Watkins, July 2023.

0
THE FOOL.

The Fool

You cannot stage me, you cannot cage me,
I perform as soon as breathe.
My expression is my impression,
I become what I believe.

Call me Jester, as I fester
in spontaneity.
As surprising as an uprising,
dawn raid of shock comedy.

A Joker's game of painted shame,
my make-up runs with smears;
displays of laughter of hereafter
are really only tears.

The shower, of this flower,
plays tricks upon the crowd.
You're thinking that I'm blinking
but my eyes conceal a shroud.

I'm no-one's fool, a star at school,
I see right through disguise.
That which you feel is yours to steal
I've shown you through my spies.

VI
THE LOVERS.

The Lovers
Pt.1: Dreams (The Wedding)

Today's very special,
I'm fuzzy inside;
a tickle of goosebumps,
an explosion of pride.

Andreea and Troy
have decided forever,
whatever the future,
whatever the weather.

There'll be the odd curveball,
there always is;
but these rings are eternal,
the 'Hers' and the 'His'.

There are dreams that fall flat,
there are dreams that stand still;
but dreams become plans
when hearts say "I will".

There are dreams made of hopes,
there are dreams that come true;
dreams become real
when hearts say "I do".

(....and when written by Stu)

Pt.2: Infatuation

There is a girl
I used to laugh and sing with
as the sun shone in the sky.
Our hearts played games of children smiling.

Then the day my girl left me standing.
She never told me why.

And all I know is,
if the Earth turns for a million years
and my spirit is roaming free,
it will be searching for her.

For I will always love my girl.

There is a beauty in the trees and the stars
and the meadows in springtime.
A summer wind, an eagle flying.

But none to touch my angel,
and her radiance sublime.

So still I wonder,
as I wander
the solitary road of the aimless traveller,
if I shall see that face again,
or search in vain forever.

For I will always love my girl.

(from Cosmic Visions, 2021)

Pt.3: Gemini and Capricorn

I don't exist outside of you.

I don't want to, even for the blink of an eye.
Would I die....
I'm certain I'd be ground with a pestle and mortar
into crumbs, into powder.

I'd surrendered my sovereignty, that very first day,
the anticipated rush,
the wave of the euphoric shiver,
the shudder, the tremor of tension.

Your arms are a cradle of autumn warmth.
Our bed, a haven from the bite of wanton winter,
a cold and icy frost, a cocoon, a chrysalis,
protected, armoured.

Where did I go?

When was the momentary switch?

Was it creeping, was it slow,
was it undiscernible, impossible to know?
No focal beam, or turning lathe of form?
Silhouette, outline, visible shape or early warning?
The bliss and elation of our very first morning.

Perhaps my urgency and electricity
forced the fateful path,
manifested in a magic of merged mind and matter.

I don't exist outside of you,
and I don't want to.

Advance, this dance, by ten insane years.
This fog of freedom and release
becomes a today from a yesterday.
I didn't notice the decadence of our decade,
our drama and our dream,
and our desperate devotion with its positive pain.

Every angstrom of distance apart
is an agonising harpoon to the heart,
though I'd still find a well

for the arrogant acid of my temper.
Your unbreakable, indestructible adoration
allows my comfort zone
to extend into psychobabbled anger,
when the kitchen bin is too full.
How dare you be that lazy.

Moments later, you find out
that I've forgotten to buy
the correct brand of sparkling water, and
the shoe switches feet with a shock,
and I face the fire and fevered fury
of your Irish and Spanish ancestors.

I love you,
and every last idiosyncrasy, so much.

Nobody should fear their life-amorous partner.
"Fear isn't useful anyway,
don't bother with it", I say,
aloofly, convincing myself I'm sounding like
Einstein, or Elon.

We're not really scared, however loud the voices.
If you never shouted at me,
or held me to account, so beautifully,
when I bellow my pointless beefs,
the fizzle-out would have ruthlessly fired
the white-hot kiln of boredom
within two lunar cycles.

Silence and howling wolves are easy to choose between,
no ponderation required.
Placidity and soft-speak
are not for war-torn warriors like us.

Gemini and Capricorn,
astral twins,
a formidable, Olympian team,
and though it was never said aloud,
the certainty was aflame in the furnace of our souls,
long before my excited, frantic stumble
on that Wiltshire road.

We just knew, everything.
Every single thing.

I don't exist without you,
and I don't want to.

(from Cataclysmic Vibrations, 2022)

XIX
THE SUN .

The Sun

Only
a lonely
small
yellow ball
of incandescent gases,
plasmasphere,
hydrogen-helium firecracker,
master-maestro,
provider,
core of masculinity....

Humanity....
has become
an inhuman,
inhumane husk;
a remnant,
a half-remembered
hallucination;
its rivers of moral authority
have run dry,
leaving no more
than parched and desolate aridity.

The electric vehicle....
a monochromatic

sales pitch of
anthropological redemption,
manufactured
salvation;
they tell us of our planet's panacea,
a technological utopia,
but it was never ours.

Internal combustion
graduates
into hazy obsolescence
before the eyes of the watching world,
transfixed in a
mesmeric trance
of Rapid Eye Movement,
blindness, and catatonia.

Obfuscation of truth
has not left us;
the marketing men
underwent a metamorphosis.
Donned a new costume.
A costume of saintly cloaks;
a voice of pseudo-wokeness,
political correctness,
a church-bowl collection
of our usurped faith.

Promises
of perceived perfection
and geo-health,
with no hint of stealth,
let alone wealth.
Evolution;
nay,
evilution!
Murderous mines
of lithium, of cobalt,
no longer secret -
genocidal
and physiological
horror.

The new battery hens.
Batteries of batteries,
for my tablet,
your phone,
our laptop,
paid for by expendable
Congolese children,
sweating to communal death,
breathing their toxic breath.

Children without faces or names,
collateral damage,

commercial desolation,
corporate decree.

As our skin roasts and bakes
from historical mistakes
that came in disguise
with false noses and lies,
camouflaged as answers....
Answers to problems we gleefully spawned.
Under illusions
that we were kings and queens
instead of pawns.

The changing climate
of the primary primate
was its own shadowy nemesis
from the dawn of its machines.
A quiet whisper behind masks
fabricated from delusion, grandeur,
and a doomed destiny
of catastrophic conclusion.

And so we hover,
like hummingbirds
and bumblebees,
suspended in inanimation.

Can what has been done, be undone?

Optimism has been the downfall
of the dreamers
throughout eternity,
as they race to replace
without loss of face, luxury or comfort,
one disastrous
trajectory of self-indulgence
with another.
The words and warnings of the wise
are deemed unworthy.
Even, and especially,
when evident demise is explained.

A Heliopolis, a bright citadel,
beaming its energies
into the mouth of the mighty Ra;
Sun God,
illuminator,
bringer of warmth and safety,
deliverer of inevitable karma,
enactor of ultimate punishment,
repayer of infinite debt,
life giver,
slow death bringer.

ACE of CUPS.

Ace of Cups

I know of an eskimo,
that was bitten by a mosquito,
because his reactions were slow.
He had to park all his money in escrow.
As above, so below,
don't be swept away by the undertow.
It'll go low,
take your legs away before you know.
But you can always go,
and talk to the eskimo.
Twenty miles East by the flight of the crow.

Honey mask and dewdrop lily,
cinnamon tree,
awakened, flightless fancy,
all invisible to me,
but felt so vividly, so acutely,
umbilical knot of genetic sorcery.
It is better for all if you do not see
what is going to be.

With your ear trumpets and binocular view,
one could be defied that you'd been there too;

is your pineal calcified,
by the fluoride,
or is that a tale told by an old wife
at the end of her life,
as a gesture of legacy and conspiracy?
Or is there veracity
in her Au Revoir of audacity?

Never trust gossip or grapevine.
They can be moronic, overly saturnine.
Whispers from China,
or cackling mynah.
A starling,
or even your dreamy darling,
because your inner child is the only entity
that won't lie to you,
and trick you,
a la Brutus.
Et tu.

XIII
DEATH.

Death
Pt.1: Frog-Eye Lens

When old things die, new things are born.
One door closes for another to open.
The Death of one era, the birth of the next.
Some say that Death is not Death,
but merely a passage into a new life,
a new being, a new beginning,
newly reborn with a new shell
but an intact, immortal soul.

There is a cycle to things.
As sure as water evaporates,
rises to become cloud,
and returns to Earth as rain;
or as plant and animal live their lives,
die, and rot, to become vulture or crow food,
everything renews and takes its place
around the circle of nature.
Death is only a point on its edge.

Unlucky thirteen? Not necessarily.
In this environment,
Death has many faces, many facets.

Renewal, the shedding of a restrictive skin
that holds back upcoming
adventure and revelation.
Not the apocalyptic vitriol of the Beast
of the Book of Revelation,
or even the Four Horsemen
that count themselves beside a pretender
that dares to call himself Death.

The Pale Rider would name himself
after the true bearer of that earth-shaking name.
A tribute. A sign of admiration,
of the omnipotence of the being
who transcends every legend
and every ancient culture.
They all bow down to the spirit
of that amorphous spectre of the underworld,
given many names and many images,
but Death is as invisible as the air.
There is no equivalent force
among all paper goddesses or gods,
no match for the unique power-set;
remover of lifebloods and commander of souls.
That power is undiminished by
the certainty that new Life follows Death,

as that is not its domain,
it passes to another.
A very singular function
but universally unmatched
or even challenged.
All back away.

The beauty of blooming flowers wilts
at a nod of the merciless head.
Crocodiles, lions and eagles know
that they are under the looming shadow
it both casts, and is.
The right hand teases until the left
swipes and takes,
without warning and without mercy.

Physical bodies are temporary homes,
lifeless cadavers even more so;
eaten, rotted, decomposed
into unrecognisable heaps of ash,
that then scatter on the wind
leaving not a trace of matter or form,
no remaining shape or substance.
Gone.

Pt.2: Phoenix Wing

A seance and a Ouija lay foundations for the truth.
Killers underpin the sacred realm from Death to youth.
Feed the hungry belly that devours the great unknown.
The price we pay for every night we gaze up at the moon.

When dim looks bright, and dark seems light,
and white is black as pitch,
each lost and roaming soul
cannot connect, or scratch its itch.
We rarely know the details of the day of our last breath,
the dice decide our destiny
with a gentle nudge from Death.

Don't trouble me with trivia, I'm trained to spot the lies,
detection is essential if we're not to compromise,
an alabaster ashtray will dispatch a feral foe;
the phoenix is but mythical.
It's crucial that you know.

There seems a cold conundrum,
the minus and the plus,

is Death a friend or enemy,
or just protecting us?
Emotions don't come into it.
The actions are detached.
And all in isolation.
Nothing is attached.

The ruthless executioner.
No reaper grim or grey.
Discharges every duty
every hour of every day.

Inside the Ouroboros ring,
perpetual and fierce,
all energy transmutes and dissipates
through grief and tears.

The eyeglass and the spyglass
are blind unto the void,
for in the magic moment
only Death is not destroyed.

XVII
THE STAR.

The Star

Life is, so simply,
sometimes nothing more
than a hell-hole of water rats,
screeching as they gnaw
at each others' chewy tails,
vainly seeking Truest North;
bleeding out in scarlet
as they scurry back and forth.

Embrace the euthanasia,
the espionage, the erasure.
Cantilever construction
of a bridge of mass destruction.
Catalysts of cyclones
and cataracts of concrete.
Wrestling with the rested;
combat with the complete.

Eye-level antennae,
that extend to an arm's length;
they detect the waves of worldliness
in an atmosphere of strength;
the orchestration of orchids,

in wretched, withered calm,
egregious intentions
lead the faithful into harm.
I'm approaching a situation,
an intangible interrogation.
Eight-limbed arachnoid crystals,
astronauts, astrophysicals.
This optical-illusory fissure
in the black ionosphere,
it cancels out our senses,
we cannot see or hear.

Geranium toothpick mantra.
Chrysanthemum spartan ellipse.
Cyanotype cyanide cytoplasm.
Total solar eclipse.
Spherical geoid in space.
Gravity balanced as one.
She is in tune with the moon.
He is in tune with the sun.

I
THE MAGICIAN.

The Magician

There's something I have to explain.
You cannot keep up with your brain.
It races in every direction
but it can't tell the sun from the rain.

So once you have understood that,
you are ready to kneel on the mat.
Empty your mind for reception.
You'll soon be as sharp as a cat.

I'm not where I am by mistake.
I learned how to bend and to break.
To always exceed expectation,
and always give more than I take.

Magic accepts without end.
Essence can always transcend.
No force, complete relaxation.
You learn how to break and to bend.

Wisdom will course through each bone.
Every idea will self-clone.
Dawnings of realisation.
The gateway to access the zone.

The Magician learns faster than all.
He stands like a tree, high and tall.
He feels every possible sensation
and dwells in the ancestral hall.

Magician and Master and Man,
plans the celestial plan,
knower of all revelation.
Follow his path if you can.

IX
THE HERMIT.

The Hermit

Sometimes in the morning, when the sun rises,
in the evening, after a heavy day,
when tumbling promises break apart loudly,
the walls and the floors a-buckling like clay.
The old man,
at the windmill,
I talk to him.
He tells me stories that carry my troubles away.

When I have questions I wish to ask,
to see and hear of the secrets of Earth,
when joy and hope have deserted me cruelly,
and I, left wondering what all things are worth....
The old man,
at the castle,
I speak with him.
He laughs with me and fills my heart with truth.

Life's jigsaw pieces strewn across the floor,
how can I start to piece them together?
The Hermit's vision is unpolluted,
he sees the elements create the weather.

The old man,
in the forest,
he tells me.
I leave his company with thoughts I keep forever.

Spirits surround us, but remain unseen,
light and darkness in tunnels of thought;
difficult choices, which do I grasp?
Wires of temptation stretched and taut....
The old man
sees sea and sky,
knows them both.
He smiles, shares his wisdom from a timeless heart.

Melting into parallel dimensions,
sights and colours take my breath away,
spiritual flights, beyond the material,
triumphant gardens, where children play.
The old man,
he lives there,
he shows me.
I feel belief that brings a brand new day.

The old man speaks to me all the time,
the voice of reason, from the astral plane.
He is a very good friend of mine,
a calming presence on a runaway train.
The old man,
within me,
he holds me.
Cradling my soul, to shield me from pain.

The old man waits there, for you and me,
telling magical tales we can believe.
My arcane guide, at my side,
my weaver of the perfect weave.
The old man
knows us.
Loves us.
Swim in the river, dissolve and breathe.

The old man is ever a mountain of love.
The old man shines in a fountain of light.
The old man burns in the rising sun.
The old man's shadow is the dead of night.

That old man,
that young boy,
that hermit.
Radiant energy.
Ecstasy bright.

X
T
A
R
O
WHEEL of FORTUNE.

The Wheel of Fortune

Fortitude favours the brave,
fortitude is the splendid, spatial,
inter-cerebral architecture,
under which gannets feast on fragments
and pick at brown carcasses,
under an incandescent sun.
Do not presume, or attempt to arbitrate,
as it is all a matter of fate,
and to lift such a weight,
though it be well worth the wait,
it is not our place or privilege
to tell the crooked from the straight.

To sit in orchard or orangery or
to watch in awe, after
the bamboo sits in deceptive silence,
protecting its secret, deceiving the sky,
before the shoots shoot upward,
with no hint of a morning warning of the hidden drama.
Sometimes, even the accuracy of a surgeon
is insufficient for the difficulty of the tasks demanded,
and one returns to nothing more
than a spin of the aphoristic, carnal wheel.

Resplendent in the most vivid colourations,
a close sibling of the bird of paradise,
who, as we are all painfully aware, will only alight
on the hand that does not grasp -
yet all the while aching for
the smallest drops
of sincerity, attention and affection.
She mocks as we snatch at her elusive perfection.
We are always under the thumbs of those we adore.
It's the tenth unwritten law.

What will be will be, it is what it is, they all say.
All laid out in unchangeable tarmac freeways,
to destinations we never saw,
but were always headed for.
That illusion of free will,
of decisions and control, of personal influence,
of goals and chases, of mastery over fate itself,
of autonomous pride and poise.
To make the cut, when they dice the meat
and separate the men from the boys.

When you roll the dice, bet on seven,
you'll be right as often as not,
it's just probability.

Chance is currency, directly and indirectly,
play the long game, not the short.

There are lacerations and copious bloodshed
along the wrong fork at the junction;
don't let any chancer convince you of anything else.
Nobody gets a real choice about anything!
Let alone a command over our futures.

The jungle's foliage can be so dense,
that only a machete clears the way
to advance but a single stride.
And as a rule, no-one carries one.
Meaning that only lateral movement is possible.
Meaning that time is devoured with voracious frenzy.
With your wind at my back I hold all the cards,
but I can't feel the air move, and so the cards are
all blank when the day is done.
I'll burn the cards, for warmth.

Scabs are ugly things, but they are omens of healing.
If we play word association, and I say "carbon",
do you picture graphite, graphene or diamond?
Or have you no knowledge of the word?

As if I'd said "iodine" or "boron"?
Glaciers barely move, but they do move,
only far too slowly to be observed.
Life is the same. Does that mean, in theory,
that we are all made of ice?
Gradually melting?
Select me, and either dissect me, or protect me.

XIV
TEMPERANCE.

Temperance

Misguided, bereft, aimless I travel,
clutching, with desperation,
at the straws of the ego, the superego, and the id.

A testosterone rush will always counter
every well-meant resolution
to live amongst the patient and the calm of temper.

At the end of the tempestuous day,
we are all at the mercy of our biochemistry;
it rules our spontaneous lives with a rod of iron.

Cobweb strands, tickling and teasing
as we walk through them in our old
and abandoned houses of murky memory,
crafted with meticulous care by busy spiders.
They are pressing on with their duties
and do not mean to frighten us.

Urges. Purges. Tinkering with promised,
eager commitments to change us

into something we are not, but yearn to be.
As if to stretch us, rubber band
or elastic from the waist of an undergarment,
only to release the tautness and ping us back to Earth.

The yogi speaks of mind control and ruthless discipline.
Despite his countenance of sublime serenity.
The focus is the key.

Maintenance. A fixed third-eye gaze
with no wavering or weakness, yet not achieved
through concentration, but the absence of.

A diamond-encrusted scabbard under the floor,
coated in dirt and grime,
to the point where it cannot be seen.

Metallic shields of fear, that aren't even here,
mask the light of the stars and the pulsars behind,
crippling doubt and confusion.

Bullets whizz past blind eyes, their aim is untrue;
do not concern yourself, or fret,
there is no place for oblique hesitation.

Obey that instinct. Trust the inner compass,
that it may override the ego's
screaming impulses, and buy the prize.

Stimulus, within signal, within motive,
relentlessly bombarding the see-saw,
forming fractal distractions and spectra.

The escaping erudition has deserted,
far past arm's length, is there any way of grasping
the silt and sand of judgement?

ACE of WANDS.

Ace of Wands

This is our flight over fanciful fences,
Luring us here under perished pretences,
Testicle cream of attacks and defences,
O carrots, sticks and the limelight.

Iris in green splits a bone from its marrow,
Mechanic's machine, or swoop of a sparrow,
Shine me away over straight within narrow
in a bare-knuckle ride to a prizefight.

Truculence teetering close to the edge
of unwashed happenstance, thin end of the wedge,
Each compass point darkened in destitute pledge,
While we dance in the shimmer of starlight.

All joking aside, there are tales to relay,
A pabulous banquet; hedonist's soiree,
I'll waver and maunder and jig on the parquet,
A mastodon, buried in midnight.

His majesty melts to a spiral montage,
Hides under mesh in scant camouflage,
Gambles a king's ransom, fain arbitrage,
In a whirlwind that rips up his birthright.

Wave the white wand as a challenge to black,
Dare them! Taunt them! Lay down the track,
Trapped, surrounded, alas and alack,
Creation of worlds in grey half-light.

IV
THE EMPEROR.

The Emperor

My mirages of idle conceit are legendary,
certainly notorious, even though
they are children of paranoid schizophrenia.
Such arrogance is either God-given, or from Fortune.

The general tolerance of a society
toward things they cannot understand,
grows lower and lower, as time goes by,
so that the ability of a brain the size of a toad's,
combined with a diet of mass-marketed snack narratives
and fabricated, funnelled content,
drops to a point where they cannot perform
the least inkling of intellectual analytics.
Instead, there's more a fever pitch
of football, celebrity scandal
and political caricatures,
delivered with pseudo-integrity.

None of this affects me.
The belief that a schizophrenic
might try to kill an innocent bystander,
for no other reason than he's a looney tune,
and thought, in that moment,

that the bystander were tiger or dragon,
fuels the fire of fear of everyone that's different.
Passing me in the street
a stranger would be none the wiser,
but if by some means they were to discover, uncover
my most special capacity,
there are going to be six seats
between us on the bus.
Not to mention the scared,
unnerved, terrified facial expression
they will suddenly and unconsciously display.

I'll move on, my beloved Messiah Complex
deserves to see the light of day,
since I am master of all I survey,
and rightly so with my exalted Celtic bloodline,
which approaches not the Royal threads
of Germany, Denmark or Greece -
lest I consult with web Ancestry,
discover my regality,
to be ridiculed, by the asinine arbitration of
seas of self-correct tabloids.

Regardless of the honest assessment of fact or reality.
There is no need for the residing bluebloods to panic –

because I, like you, have less than zero interest
in living in a palace, or castle,
unable to walk in freedom around an ancient monument
that my ancestors built from distant stones of
elephant-skin hue.

Or a supermarket,
without a team of sunglassed bodyguards in tow.
It's no recipe for a happy, wholesome,
fulfilled existence,
no matter how much wealth
and artificial, ludicrous pomp and status
are attached to the harlequinade.
The costumes, gold and pageantry offend my eye too,
give me colourful, pagan-minstrel, festival attire, any time.

It's best, when you're in charge,
through the kind of occult manipulation
that even Machiavelli himself could never approach,
not to broadcast what you know
and how you know it;
your secret societies, your arcane knowledge,
equipping you with opportunities, skills,
for the purpose of influencing the influential,
individuals, the world, in clandestine rooms of fairytale.

No further shall I refer here to such trifles, sacraments,
in their silent, forbidden, succulent, delicious detail.

I use social media far less than I once did,
and the reasoning for that - is that -
hovering, circling, vulture plagiarists -
thieves of intellectual property, of wise thought -
dwell in the eaves, the rafters and the walls,
in their quest for titbits, ideas, theories,
and persuasive arguments of greater greys.
One's flippant release of a small golden nugget
into the river of language soup
would soon surface, downstream,
under the highwayman-persona of a 'respected columnist'
or establishment-rag 'exclusive story'.

However, having one's words copied or stolen
is the flattery of a distilled precious metal of wisdom itself,
as the egos, glories and limelight of those
that will claim the origins
were never of real value in the first place.
Let the cuckoos bask in empty, hollow sunshine.
I move in the shadows of the secrecy.
I watch you, and everything you do, from there.

While revealing a morsel or two,
I'm drawn to deviate to a related,
historical experience.

When locked in a psychiatric ward,
an environmental caricature reminiscent of
'One Flew Over the Cuckoo's Nest'
things are noticed.
It's all those others that are unwell,
I, the attentive scrutiniser, fly on the wall.
Sheepish compliance is part of the hierarchical dynamic,
because, as in life, in society,
in the workplace, other places,
one must be seen to obey the system
so as to operate within the system.
Naturally there are many ways
to survive outside of the system -
but a psych ward is not the place to attempt that.

I too became an actor.
Concentration enabled me to assume control
over aspects of my world, and the wider world.
I manufacture ripples in the ether, either
through thought, or by casting words
and comments into space,

on waves and equations
of action and reaction,
of cause and effect.

The result of my application of these attributes?
To effect changes,
storyline propaganda will urge me
to inject matters into a surgically pinpointed
area of the internet,
the word-swamp of cultural domino-topple,
to then watch the ripples move away from me,
back into my arena,
manifested and moulded.
Chaos and order, appropriately juxtaposed.
I am beyond the eyes of the revelate
if my movements are not understood by my adversary,
should they seek to formulate
opposition, scapegoat and subversive strategy.
The Art Of War.

There are, you would hope, borders to my empire,
edges of where I reach boundaries to my limitations.

There is no temptation or compulsion
to sit on a beach and bark orders at the sea.
No desire to embarrass myself, or commit suicide
by jumping from a high building
with only wax adhering my wings.
My limits work for me,
and they also work for me,
in both senses.

I use my gifts of dominance when and where I am able,
when I judge there is purpose to.
I am happy betwixt those glass statues.
No human possesses
more access or aptitude in asymmetric view,
why would I ever relinquish the monster of absolutes?

And now, if you'll excuse me,
I need to take delivery of a wonderful set
of New Clothes, for my celebratory parade.

XX
JUDGEMENT.

Judgement
Pt.1: Calculation

There are two contexts to the popular use
of the word Judgement. Traditional and Old Testament
references centre around the notion of a trial before God,
after death, where our obedience of the
rules of our faith is reviewed. We enter
the gates of eternal bliss or are damned
to the fires of Hell for ever.

This concept of Judgement Day, I have pondered
endless times, and so in my sanctuary of atheism,
my impregnable protective shell,
I decide that there is no Judgement Day.

I shall speak now
of the second popular context of Judgement.
Those personal judgements that frame the decisions
we make, in our lives,
travelling the twists and turns of our journey's roads.

We make our value judgements by applying intellect,
experience, knowledge and wisdom to

situations; decisions;
and the belief systems we
subscribe to.
The belief systems themselves are
altered by others,
if our resolve is weak and easily overpowered.

Pt.2: Projection

Oh! Don't set and chase goals; it's so....Western.
Face East: adopt productive habitual behaviours.
How you spend your time, live the process,
not a wish list of desired purchases.
One works, brings rounded sense of purpose,
that which the Japanese call Ikigai,
while the other does neither, in any lasting way.

The most vital thing in your life,
and your being,
is to recognise
what is important and what is not - to YOU.

Musicians, writers, architects, artists, touch immortality.
Living forever on in their mustard creations.

Ideas float by on the passing river.
We scoop them out when we see them
or they float by, disappear, for ever.
Two build a relationship, invariably, one ends it.
Believe, and become.

I used to be sad that I was sad.
I'm much happier happier.
It is always better to create than copy, if you can.
If you cannot, it's a priceless thing to learn.

Each moment shows a decision,
each decision is a door.
A door that then will close itself
for now and evermore.

The only things that are real about time,
are that we have a limited amount of it,
and we are always unaware of how much we have left.

We must ruthlessly own our lives.

Television is a device of distraction,
designed to eat time and attention, so that
we do not use our brains for
unwelcome, inconvenient purposes.

I plant seeds, of all kinds, every day,
and nurture those already sown.
It brings me happiness, joy, and
a busy and beautiful garden.

Is philosophy anything more than sets of opinions?
Discuss.

Is a philosopher no more than a salesman of ideas?
Discuss.

Learn how to never waste a thought.
(If you succeed, you'll be the first)

A large and powerful brain is of little use
if it is not matched by your heart.

'Memes' on social media would be
a lot more accurate if they began
with the word 'sometimes'.
But that would require integrity, and Judgement.

Those that say
“we can’t do anything about the media”
were convinced of that by the media.
People that say
“we can’t do anything about the media”
forget that it is our money and attention
that is their oxygen.
I withdrew mine over a decade ago.

A gut instinct,
without a well of appropriate
experience, will be a poor guide.

In our well-meaning attempts to educate,
we may give too much information
to minds that cannot process it.

Every day is full of energy and opportunity.
It is not connected to, nor dependent upon,
phases of the moon,
or matching numbers in the date.
We get one stab at this fantastic lifetime;
we use it or lose it.

Ignore people that dispute that, too.

One of the primary functions of governments
is to hide their true functions.

The best piece of advice I've heard is
"do not search for your ideal partner, but
learn to be the ideal partner for someone else."
Often we look through the
wrong end of the telescope,
and are confused by what we see.

I try to be the best version of myself,
and then tomorrow, like all new days,
I'll try to be a little better.
Is there another way to live?

I try to fix things. I can't always do it.
But the trying, that is essential.

Fans of pseudosciences like astrology,
when challenged with facts, and the assertion

that science has taught us so much since the
times of those long-outdated beliefs,
will simply argue to discredit science itself.
As if they sit in a place high above logic
and can redefine what a fact is,
informed by a 'source' within a meme.

It is best not to send
a friend request to Facebook's algorithms.
They are nobody's friend.

Your ego, too, is not your friend,
but it is not illegal to kill it.
Try.

The establishment are unafraid
of social media traffic,
by design it only amounts to swamps
of white noise and confusion,
for the hapless and hopelessly addicted.

Arguing with strangers on social media
is like pissing in the sea,
and waiting for the water to change colour.

Pt.3: Iconoclasm

Our lives are only accumulations
of decisions, each made
upon the foundations
of the temples of our Judgement.

V
THE HIEROPHANT

The Hierophant

In all of us, there is a fascination with the obscure,
a preoccupation with hypnotic mystery.
For each of us, there is one above all others,
glowing with his incandescent aura of history.

Some will call him sage, or mystic,
elder of the ancestral line;
some will call him mage, or muse,
or weaver of the faeries' twine.

Guardian of secrets, hiding the forbidden,
keeper of abstraction, holder of the hidden.
Consultant to the curious, revealer of divinity,
opener of gateways, marked with masculinity.

He has walked in mist with angels, flown with snowy owls,
shuffled with sidewinders, shared the leopards' prowls.

His many names forgotten long ago,
'Hero' they now say.

He smiles for when he was such a thing,
a dim and distant day.

Sigils, carved into titanic boulders,
sentinels, marking and protecting
entrances and exits with coded passwords,
daubed in blood, and warpaint of woad,
harbouring curses and spells
in prehistoric, barbarian languages,
are the gauntlets of challenge
thrown at the trespassing feet
of infidel intruders.

Sealed, impregnable chambers
beckon the enquirers,
entice their impatience.
Our Hero,
with his blunt spear, serpentine staff,
taps rhythmically upon the surface of the flint,
and of its own volition
it rolls to the Southern side.

Within, one might expect to see
the Holy Grail,

Ark of the Covenant,
or a diamond like the Koh-I-Noor;
but instead we see books,
seemingly bound in the flesh of pachydermal animals,
miraculously well-preserved,
one can barely imagine
what their origins and contents could be.

A convoluted, labyrinthine,
egalitarian frontage
of grisly, sketched,
indecipherable writings,
and characters,
which, to untrained eyes,
are no more possible to decode
than the Voynich Manuscript.

The Hero is as old as time.
Ask him of the rarest
and most perfect mathematics.
Ask him to tell of the
insights of lost philosophers.
He fights his cerebral battles
on other, inaccessible
planes of consciousness.

He is he. And not me.
But there is a fulcrum of spacetime,
a crossover, a Mobius strip,
where the two flip,
and the Inner Hero
finds an inner voice,
and then he becomes me.
It's not a blip, it gets a grip.

I have my Outer Hero and Inner Hero,
my Outer Hierophant and Inner Hierophant,
they whisper into my ancient ears
when they know I need them to.

ACE of PENTACLES

Ace of Pentacles

When this cornerstone of sarcasm and inverse opulence
appears at a focal point in a reading,
beware the temptation to trust it
as an omen of windfall or wealth.
Once it has turned eleven times from eleven,
maybe the Fates have genuine smiles on their faces -
but not before.
Restrain your urgency
to follow a rainbow that has no end, and no gold.
An ace can also be an apex,
or an arrow aimed the artwork of Artemis.

Apollo will ask you to act as the arbiter
between anger and agreement.
Afterburn will bring
argument and acidity.
Apoplexy, with its
arrogance and amputations,
will arm the archers in the assumption
of aptitudes, attitudes and altitudes.
Apples and pears are to be expected,
atop the asterisks at the angular aperture,
above the stairs,
or those similarly affected.

Pay attention to the
artistry of the applicable arithmetic.

It will not serve you well
to read the signs as they appear,
I have stated this shortly before;
you'd do far better to search for more,
at the starting gun or the hardware store.
It would assist you, too, to block the door.
Jam the jamb.
Put the ace in the hole.

We have a Houdini in the house.
Approach him and he'll turn in on himself
like a woodlouse.
So, keep your distance.
With luck, you'll have found an ally.
If not, there'll be no small amount of trouble.
Make your moves with care.
Try keeping everything slow
every time you come or go,
every time you stop and go.
Dig deep, and don't sleep.
If you do, you will see no glimpse of tomorrow.

Orienteering is the sport you want to learn,
should you think you'd like to feel the burn.
Take a crossbow and not a pistol,
to draw no chance vibration of quartz crystal.
This ace is impatient and fast;
don't worry that the fight is going to last.
It isn't.

There's a cyclops, and he's staring at a point.
His nose has been knocked laterally out of joint.
Infuriate the giant if you dare,
but he'll flay you and take your scalp. He likes hair.
Extendable horizons slice the sky;
expendable collateral, sell or buy.

A Sword, a Wand, a golden Cup or Coin,
the aces high above fall in Des Moines.
In Iowa, Hiawatha cuts the throats,
the corpses pass the time in lonely boats.

XVI
THE TOWER.

The Tower

The little white Ford Escort, with a diesel engine,
that the company has allowed me to borrow,
brings me to Norfolk, a top-notch hotel,
and a room with a jacuzzi,
in a semi-blizzard of quickly settling snow.

It's my birthday, a fresh-faced twenty-nine,
this Capricorn of January,
such a dream state, a vision, a skyward line.

Turning points in life, you feel them
as they appear over the horizon,
their energy and force,
their thrust, their muscles in line,
the gallop of a Palomino horse.

The new professional family,
welcoming, beckoning,
acceptance, trust and faith,
no inkling of the omen of shadow,
the blackened presence of the waiting wraith.

I have the blood of the bull,
the strength of the ox,
the charge of the ram;
enveloping my being, feeding my belly,
reminding me exactly who I really am.

I'm not to dream, or guess, foresee,
or dare to draw a plan,
that I'll fall in false love, twice, in the space of weeks,
as if my destiny were to clear a fresh path
and mould a new man.

Patience is a virtue,
as everyone becomes so acutely aware,
Monday morning surprise birthday cake,
a genuine gesture of accepting care.

Lisa, pretty, funny, able to
hide effortlessly in a crowded room,
so easy to be with and laugh with,
even with a black rose of obsession
lurking, threatening to bloom.

The summer is so hot this year,
as are the sales results of the high-flying team.
If I could see around corners,
I might steer a course to dodge the extreme.

I awaken to a blazing, sunny dawn,
in fear of an imaginary foe; it's a bright 6am,
I call Lisa to warn her
so she knows I'm afraid of 'them'.

I'll head to Wiltshire, to my home town,
I'll be safe, I'll hide, I'll lay low,
a four hour drive, usually, but an engine fail
and twelve-mile walk make it tortoise-slow.

My parents' home is locked, why?
They're on holiday in the USA!
I'll call a friend, put my psychosis on display,
so my well-paid job can be taken away.

Journeys into ourselves are wondrous, joyous,
but less so when they destroy,

from the inside the view is a kaleidoscope,
it whistles and whirls,
my grown man is a wide-eyed, frightened boy.

A calamitous switch, thrown in a
hidey-hole, in a human brain,
the most advanced creation in nature,
turns and twists the world on its head
and breaks it, to spawn an alien creature.

My life is to end and start anew,
and once I can grasp the gifts it bestows,
my inner Lazarus will rise,
before their damning eyes,
that classic door will open, let the old one close.

III
THE EMPRESS.

The Empress

The icon of femininity, of maternity,
extends and envelops all,
from the macroscopic to the microscopic,
and every fragment of the fusion
basks in the milk of Empress.

As far as Western medicine can yet reach,
it is not far enough,
to explain why at some point in utero,
a growing and duplicating, multiplying morass,
a blob, of developing matter,
precipitates a leap of its life
when the first heartbeat instantaneously arrives.
Our earthly, mortal genius is embarrassed;
pants down in front of the class,
red-faced and tearful in its hopelessness.
Eastern teachings, tribal legend, ancient lore,
explain the riddle and solve the mystery.
It tells us, in its empirical simplicity,
as if it should be obvious to the least able child,
that the first heartbeat is nothing more - nor less -
than the exact moment when the soul enters the body.

That, in the perfect, coinciding, magical energy
of the clicking of The Empress' fingers,
in initiative, pious decree.
She begins all life at her divine chosen moment,
not before, and not after.

For the embryo,
cocooned in its liquid safety and protection,
it feels like a squirt of energy
in the space directly below the heart,
and a jolt as the electrical impulse
ignites the beginning of sentience,
the dawn of notion of truth, sacred life,
and the awakened soul.

As we stumble and bumble through our lives,
she sits, perpetually, upon our shoulders,
watching and waiting
at every mistake, venture, experiment,
guess, hunch, battle, attack, defence, lesson,
wound of blade and graze of knee.

VII
THE CHARIOT.

The Chariot

Indelible markings and precise
sacred geometry unfold themselves,
perfect archaic symbols,
written in blue-black ink on sandstone walls.
Be the echo,
the reaction to the weight of anger,
or a whispering sprite
that dances like vertigo melodies
on a carousel of whirling, mesmeric music.

Anchoring oneself to a security blanket
of soft, comfortable childhood toys
in shadows of embraces,
envelop the spirit of mocking deceit,
and cruel translucent illusions
of shallow ponds of happiness
in lucid, crystalline shriek-metal.

The reflection blurs. The outlines merge
into symmetrical design, and paint outlines of darkness
over the psychological diagram.
It is impossible to detect with a mere five senses,
that all sprays of vision give a pure absence

of clarity, definition and depth of image;
hint and matter or crisp,
battle-scarred permanent unhealable wounds
destroy any subtlety of shade.

We fail to notice, or realise, fissures and ravines
splitting our every perception
of the universes of time and space,
those governing commanders
that issue diktats upon orders and instructions
which we casually defy and deny.
Hollow deity and imaginary ghost
with their formless, invisible,
worthless attempted controls,
vanish, with nothing more
than a singular switching thought,
notion or fragile belief.
The canvases are blank.

If the marksman blinks,
the stag, even the rabbit remain free
and are safely out of range once again.
The speed of a thought or an idea
hits the cerebral cortex with such tardiness
that dimensionality will reverse, and upend,

before a decision or a choice
can even begin to materialise,
let alone be processed.
Observe how instantaneously
a honeycomb-eyed housefly
reacts to the fastest of nimble predators,
and is gone within a lightning flash.

The spleen-wrench moves in flame-fire
and flutters as the wing of a swallow.
Dive-bombing like a falcon,
splashing like a salmon
climbing waterfalls upstream,
hearing the apparent silences
that equip a bat to negotiate space
in the blackness of pitch,
dwarfing humanity into sludge and tar.
Opposable thumbs
are insignificant trump cards
under such stark scrutiny.
Man is mouse.

A long and laboured line
stand with longbows taut,
resembling the anticipation

expressed by hapless fish below
the scooping paw of the brown bear.
The vain darting of the frantic zebra,
spying a vicious leopard
that has already accelerated to unstoppable velocity,
and whose life is seen before it
in the span of a second.
It cruelly witnesses and smells its own spilt blood,
hears and feels the tearing of its own flesh,
before the lights go out.

The Chariot displays countless truths
to the eye that pays enough of
the keenest kinds of attention,
of focus, direction, concentration,
of desire, curiosity,
interpretation, of computation.
It reveals nothing to the blind,
the ignorant, or the shallow.
Umbrellas of scorn and disdain
are the shields upon which the rain cascades,
and rebounds back to a skyward trajectory,
scattering into puddles of flat water.

Equations on a page.
The trained mind speaks the language,
the untrained mind may as well
be peering at a sheer black space.
Show me. I have a ball of crystal.
Tell me. How the knowledge flows.
Teach me. Wisdom of the ancients.
It is my birthright, my destiny, my inheritance.
The mathematics. The manuscripts. The mystery.
To crawl on a silver-coloured tablecloth,
escaping from lime-green and olive-green catfish,
clouded vision due to a dense, grey fog
that comes up from the flat of the floor.
Has there been a spill of oil?
Take the October train to the summit
of the craggy granite peak,
and turn to gaze at the underbelly of Hades.

The aromatic stench of petroleum
reaches through membrane,
to osmose in the direction
of a lurking yellow chariot,
wind-fast, ominous, portentous, ferocious.
There is no need to bat an eyelid.
The water is calm. The water is cool.
Loitering in that tiger suit won't convince anyone.

It's incrimination by stealth and subterfuge.

We are sheltering from storms,
abused pawns,
the landscape of thorns
is impossible to cross,
except for the airborne;
bird, flying insect
or pollen on the breeze.
Why, why is this unfolding?
Mutually assured but not
mutually exclusive destruction?
Powerless gods?

Annihilation at the hands of a lunatic fringe?

Answers will evade, eternally.

The Chariot and its damaged undercarriage
are in a defective state.
There isn't a destination,
there isn't a conclusion,
and there is no defined date.

Do not cling, limpet-like,
to the rock's surface
as waves crash and break around you,
to dislodge you, to displace you.
The seeds of the end-of-the-world flowers
were sown long ago, did you not know?
They look pretty.
Little Red Riding Hoods,
growing in snow,
but with snarling and carnivorous jaws
and teeth underneath.
Pilots plotted deadly courses,
passengers willingly and consciously travelled,
despite a clear and horrific view
of the beckoning doomsday ahead.

Is it worth heading North?
Is it best to go West?
The priest points East,
but the river's mouth is to the South.
We can choose to stay, stagnate,
avoid every junction
and invitation to adventure,
bow to fear,
obey uncertainty;
tread water,

hesitate and delay.
If I can clear the log jam,
the clogged arteries,
the stodge of ectoplasm,
the blockages of my neural pathways
and their warm familiarity,
then perhaps there is a passage beyond,
to a glade of beauty
and an enlightened breaking dawn.
A place where an open heart
and open mind
are a gateway to a future
of trance and obscure magnetism.

Kinetic or static,
energy or electricity,
moon-fire or sun-fruit nectar,
psychic dream or emotional, subatomic force,
all are a conundrum
in the arbitrary panacea
of bliss-encased ecstasy.
None of the related channels
lead anywhere interesting,
unless for the execution
of warrants and contracts that tie
one sphere of galactic awareness to another.

Alone in the fear-bubble,
suspended in limbo,
hovering in temporary balance
in static gravity,
floating gyroscopic dust
settled within cocoons of mercury and uranium,
we children of the cosmos
slide into empty tunnels like effluent waste.
They're encrypted in codes at the molecular level,
just like the nucleic acids in biochemistry,
twisted into bio-solutions
at breakneck speeds.

Warriors bleed.
They watch as it pours and drains away
before their own eyes,
and they press on the wound
until the liquid traffic desists.
The crack and crunch of fracturing bone
is the rhythmic drum pattern,
while the cartilage and muscle
tear in motifs of tuneful harmony.

The Chariot is the vessel
that moves between the cards.

As fluid as air or water
and as grounded as fire or earth,
it can be
everywhere or nowhere,
nothing or something,
finite or infinite,
but uniform of presence.
Positive, negative or neutral.
Open, closed.
Transparent, opaque.
White hot, ice cold.
All energy and matter
in one place or all places,
The Chariot carries any and all things.

ACE of SWORDS.

Ace of Swords

A sword so sharp and substantial
that it could cleave a man in two,
from crown of head to crotch,
with a single strike.
Who could wield such a mighty blade?
A warrior so fearsome
that none dare speak his name,
for it is said that to do so brings
a terrible curse down on the
bloodline of the offender.
One does not test the
credence of such a story.

I might only carry one weapon today,
but there have been many in my past years.
My adversarial tool of choice, presently, is
Excelsior, brother blade to Excalibur.
Majestic, metallic monster of moon-metal,
hammered out with Martian mallets on
misted marble anvils. And, as we all know,
removing a sword from its sheath
commands that it draw blood.

This meanest of means of inflicting flesh-damage
still pales in the shadow of its true purpose
and intention, which is not to maim or murder,
but instead to hack and hew
through undergrowth and overgrowth,
to clear an unfettered path of access.
Access to clarity, access to vision,
access to a sublime future.
See the coming tribulations, trials....and triumphs.

II
B
J
THE HIGH PRIESTESS

The High Priestess

O Priestess, my Priestess,
I apologise, on behalf of our species,
for the misguided men
that have somehow decided
that they hold a superior place in the world
than the fairer, feminine beings.

The lies and dogmatic doctrines
that would laughably have us believe
that Woman was fashioned
from a rib of Adam,
rather than an Adam appearing
from the loins of an Eve.

We are humbled, and we are sorry,
and we ask your forgiveness,
for our wretched transgressions.

The High Priestess bears a solemnity of power
that Man cannot begin or hope to comprehend,
and so he does not comprehend.
She, in her divine wisdom and beauty,

commands all men
through all women.

She reflects the eyes of Isis, of Nefertiti,
Cleopatra, Freya, Hera and Aphrodite.

She possesses a wrath,
an elemental command,
as colossal and wide
as anything ever fathomed or imagined
by mortal or immortal mind or spirit.

Yet those are counterbalanced
with a maternal mercy as deep,
and as expansive,
as all Poseidon's waters.

She nurtures, nourishes and cares for
all the deepest and darkest
depths and reaches of us.
She taught Aphrodite
everything she knows about love.

She teaches Man
of the ways and secrets of love;
some listen and are attentive,
while others snap in obstinacy
and arrogant, oblivious fantasy.

Her arms, that stretch to and around eternity,
embrace the planetary orbits
as they accept the vast totality of the universe.

Secrets of witches,
sacred intuition and foresight,
treasures of ancestors,
seeds of stardust,
moonmaiden and wolfscreams,
all below the dark canopy of her violet cape.

Pull my internal intuition up and beyond
into my frontal lobe, allow me
to draw peace from your
deep motherly protection,
that I may feel your transcendent enlightenment,
that I may know all that you know.

Make me the very most of me.
Make me everything I can be.
When I concentrate,
relax and release,
let me learn from
the well of your immeasurability.

O Priestess,
we surrender our priapic souls to you,
we believe in and belong to you.

We bathe in, and absorb,
your omnipresent, safe, cosmic love.

So mote it be.

XXI
THE WORLD.

The World

Me? I see the world through eight keen I's. Intuition, insight, intelligence, intellect, instinct, inspiration, imagination and integrity.

Thus opens openness. We bow in reverence to all above and before us. You've heard word of wormholes, portals and gates, unexplained in detail, forbidden galaxies, starseeds and shimmering beings, those legends and stories are wrong. Turn over this card in upright form and reveal lines, channels, multiple spokes of a wheel of scream-beam. Be ready for macrocosms and microcosms of perspective, for in this realm they are one and the same, an inverted emerald palace transcending matter and substance but as tangible and solid as stone. Allow them to enter, there is nothing to fear, not here. It will come through, to you. You will come to see, through me. I am analysing myself and my insignificance. My anachronism, my anonymous stardom, my upside-down celebrity, I reach around embarrassingly to pat my own back in a pointless gesture of shining peacock-vanity. Nobody is going to notice; it is highly probable that one day's sales of the Daily Mail or Telegraph, perhaps graced with the lofty literary skills, advanced grey-matter wit and withered warblings of overweight Old Etonian narcissists, or the multitudes of money-grabbers and social-climbing societal judges, that plant themselves in the path of the bastions of truth and honour, at the British Broadcasting Corporation over breakfast; one day of drivel-patter outnumbers all the sales of everything I'll ever write. It doesn't matter; because a writer that is not writing primarily for him or herself is not honestly writing at all. The creative mind is a bracing, turbulent ocean that never takes rest. I am semi-outcast for all I write or say, and it makes me proud. It is immaterial whether it is fair or unjust, because fairness and justice are far more common than all the propaganda pumps insist is the case. A form of obedient hypnosis and conditioning, a la Pavlov's Dog.

Take this energy, and opportunity, to place your forehead on the card of The World, on the table. Begin breathing more deeply as you go. Place your hands on the table on either side of your head, keeping your glabella in constant contact with The World. Breathe yet more deeply and for longer each time. Now, feel your feelings, experience them, interact with them. The pulses and cracks that drive the ebb and flow of high consciousness and spirit, feel them and be with them. They are coursing outward and inward through Third Eye mysticism, you must fully surrender so that you may join with them in totality. Upon connection, which you will immediately recognise and feel in that moment of merging and engaging, offer no resistance. Let it come. Embrace the force and the love that are also embracing you, as a sibling, a family member, bonded by blood and by time. If you feel weightless flotation, you are at the arrival at source energy and frequency; at one with seeker spirituality. Answers to time-trapped hidden questions are reaching for your core. It is a place of sublime safety. Of arrival. Be with it. You are discovering now. You are not, are never, too old to be young.

Retreat back to the womb-low. To dreamstate. You are an Yggdrasil branch, connected to the Nine Worlds, eternity running through every vein and vessel, blood of Gaia. Wait. Stay. All is all. Time is flat. Energy is a sea. Now transmit, receive, and be. Feel that profound and profane power, and the potency of primal wisdom that manifests in this unapologetic whole of stardust realms. There is no need to assert control. You are the object and not the subject. Let go.

You will sense when the experience lets go of you, it knows the when. See and feel a pinhole, its intensity is as hot and bright as white fire. The illumination is holding out a celestial hand for you to accept and reach out to. All of this is happening in a middle-world room that is ungoverned and untouched by the superficial illusions of space and time. There are no tangible boundaries here with real or familiar meaning or that can be described with earthly language. Everything has been merged. This is the place. The union and unity of music, meditation and mathematics that we touch and sense in dreams and subconscious thought, that we hear of and long for, that we hope is not just myth but some elusive multi-dimensional reality, hidden deep down in our inner essence, and our psyche, and our immortal soul-ectodrama.

You're wondering if you've died, whether this is where we all come to at Journey's End, inside an Ayahuasca-revelation or DMT-trip to nowhere and everywhere, believing that you can't possibly return because that's how it all feels. A mystery that you've teleported to, that doesn't exist because you're so certain it doesn't, though you know it's impression and not certainty. Space and time seem to have vanished. Just gone. There is no danger. The detachment is not a threat, incredible though that seems. Do not put a cap or a lid on it, let it rise, rise, rise. You sit in the seat of the intellect. In the seat of overlaps of the cards of the Tarot. The Tarot's identities, their symbolism and true esoteric high-awareness.

The World brings, carries and guards burning beacons of ecstatic hope, and optimistic delivery of divine connections to universal spirits and forgotten deities. Equilibrium of Yin and Yang, opposites in balance, romance of notions of Pleiadian and Arcturian starseeds and dimensions, even if they are as fictional as the fairytales of the Loch Ness Monster or Doctor

Who; Satan, God, Odin, Set or Cthulhu. Those whispered higher waves, or those eight immortal eyes I spoke of, that we carry, depend on and serve, as they loyally serve us. It is a battlefield of electromagnetic wavelengths from radio waves to gamma rays and everything in between, from the visible to the invisible.

Where is sympathy? Empathy? Compassion? Humanity? Kindness? Contentment? How about love? Understanding? We can view the card of The World as the one that represents the longest distance of message travel. Billions of light years from sources of light in our night sky, that are no longer even there, transmitting anything at all. We'll need to have another look in a billion or two years from now to establish that. Let's look forward to doing that.

It is of bittersweet and melancholy significance, though against a backdrop of profound positivity and pure synchronised coincidence, that I write these words on the day of the passing of Queen Elizabeth II; that sees end, immediately becoming beginning, unwitnessed before by almost every one of us. A moment of joyous hope that from stoic tradition and history may spring eternal a fountain of transformation. An era of a monarch of the people. A turning of tides. A duty of real care. An atmosphere of familial loyalty, right up to, and down from, the summit of a glorious shared Good Samaritan's mountain. A double rainbow omen encircled the sky. Followed smartly by deafening thunderclaps, that mirrored 96 cannon blasts of tribute and farewell, as if to remind us all of the polarity and poverty of The World we observe and inhabit, with its unbearable intensity of prejudice, pain, brutal destruction and crushing irreversible damage.

A seismic cultural shift, one hopes, boring into our indestructible, mortal hearts with metaphysical drills of diamond. The new figurehead is a man of strong opinions and convictions, but what interplay of the traditional and the trailblazer will we see take its apparitional shape as this new journey opens up before us? The champion of progressive causes or the respecter of old-fashion? The pioneer of the future or the sceptre-waver of the past? The first speech nodded ominously toward the latter but we know for certain that the former is alive somewhere inside both the man and his new machine. Which Platonic solid will this leadership resemble, Tetrahedron, Octahedron, Dodecahedron or Icosahedron? Man of the people or ruthless tyrant behind a friendly smile? The price payable for hesitation or indecision could not possibly be higher, in these times of climate emergency, though we do know that the 'point of no return' was passed more than 30 years ago, and that strategies and tactics of 'damage limitation' are all that remain as our options.

We can expect no charitable transfer of penny or pound, from that obscene and colossal estate into the hands of peasants. I dare to even imagine it and incessant ridicule will rain down upon my upstart brow. Equity seeps not between the cultural flagstones, and never shall it be.

Like the pinnacle of the Yuletide tree or the monarch of the state, The World's place in the Tarot and its reach appear as astronomical tentacles wrapped around the planet, to protect like a loving cuddle or constrict like a mighty anaconda. The World represents farthest distance and closest proximity. Highest summit and deepest abyss. Once in a while synchronicity announces its alignment, either subtly or slapped around our faces like a Monty Python fish. Queenie was a 'nice person' and epitome of faithful service; yet surely what we need from a king is leadership by example, a cradle for the poor and the freezing, and the legitimate removal of the inverted commas from the presently hypocritical term of 'United Kingdom'. There's an illustrious book about it....
Can it become worthy of the name, for the first time in the eyes of the many as well as the few?

As for the 'elites' - how about that for an oxymoron - one can easily foresee the inevitable demise of those metaphorical tail-lights as they fade away into dark oblivion, never to be seen again.

Dare the downtrodden dream of obsolesity of the ostentatious ogre-class? Of revival, of regulation, of ritual banishment? Paradoxical as it may appear, understanding of the universe is unassailable without a self that is acutely aware, in possession of high enlightenment, that at certain uncommon moments allow an energetic and magnetic pulse that enters at the base of the spine and rushes vertically from Root Chakra to Crown Chakra in four seconds of orgasmic rush.

The green Lamborghini parked quirkily on the council estate is clearly an alien presence. It sits, tempting vandalistic fate, teasing the local human magpies, for a few short days before its wheels and interior trinkets are removed in surreptitious silence, between the hours of 3am and 4am. A souvenir factory for brief amusement. The owner learns the hard way that the contracts and rules of the social strata operate in ways he hadn't guessed at. We can peer at our peers with relative impunity but there are lines you cannot cross without consequences of regret. And regret is a malignant tumour. It is a weight that gets heavier with the passing of hours until the pain is unbearable. One has only to learn to put it down on the floor when one needs to, but the way to do that has obstacles in its path that one must master. Regret is an optional, avoidable mindset.

'Society' and 'community' are in a free-fall flat-spin of decline and decay but the methods are not made visible to the naked eye, and though the origins are tweaked with malicious intent, the scapegoats are selected and blamed carefully and they are managed and moulded by careful students of Sun Tzu and Machiavelli, so nothing is what it appears to be. Concealed behind insidious lie after manufactured narrative storyline, the mud is made much muddier; as ever, helped by the regularity of our legendary British rainfall.

It feels like inhaling thick swarms of aphids, deep down into our lungs, so they are able to eat us alive from our insides out. All on an inherited farm, that our forefathers worked on, later engulfed by a pension fund. It's that simple, that moribund, that empty and devoid of heart. People attend churches, in case threats of unending chambers of torture and fire for stepping out of line are true. To deposit coins or notes in gratuity receptacles to buy our souls, in case we had inadvertently sold them to the malevolence of Mephistopheles when we weren't paying proper attention, or looking in the right direction. The liquid metal mercury architecture. Bubbling, babbling brooks of barren boredom offer flatulent welcomes, there is rumoured to be a Supreme Being taking care of us, while we chase and clamour for shallow and vacant fame, claiming our apparent divine entitlements of material gains and chocolate trophies.

I am only the incumbent occupant of this soluble body, it's temporary and frankly near to useless, as it does parts of its required tasks but mostly to a primitive level. The heir's becoming King, that's what's a-happening, in a nutshell. Asparagus is cooking, by boiling it in water on the Aga, a cast-iron heavy duty luxury appliance for chocolate-box thatched cottages covered in roses. Fragrant abundance. The rose and the cross of folklore, impossible to access or even locate, until it was decided that a website be built in place of secrecy, exclusivity and elitist doctrine. I wonder how much malignant regret has been spawned by that. Rosicrucians and Freemasons cast exclusivity aside, and advertise to attract anybody and everybody into their once-elite ranks.

Those labelled as narcissists, and those that argue with the trans lobby, are the scapegoats of the day, there are laws punishable by cancellation and bullying if we think the wrong things, hold opinions that the lynch mobs will hunt us down for and punish us with psychological torture, tearing down walls that we needed to hide behind for preservation of our sanity. No punishment is too severe for socially forbidden thoughts. Free speech is conditional. Yet common sense is prevailing, the corner turned, ambiguous ideas of biology replaced by the bedroom mirror and undeniable hormonal drives. The invention of a new chapter of anatomical definition rejected out of sheer self-evident logic and eyesight. The evidence in the mirror is a lie to every child, we were told. The truth once again has reset the smashed compass.

A lone mammoth squeezes the Maltese cheese, shoots the breeze. Crash, bang, wallop, you can hear those cannon in Timbuktu, out with the old, in with the new. All are guilty without charge, without trial. The smell is horrific, everybody pukes in the village square, and the suffocating stench is everywhere, a clapperboard snaps and a camera rolls, all the comments and traffic are written by trolls, while we each learn how to walk on red-hot coals. Our teachers mumble incoherently in Esperanto. A language that no-one speaks. Orchids sprout from the soil, scattering fortune cookies to the perimeter of the soft meadow, read them, they'll bring you life-clues, it's a nature reserve so be natural. Walk in, take free membership of the club, it's not a museum, you won't incriminate yourself if you stick to the script and make sure to steer clear of the juniper. Which musical instrument do you play? Now, take notes and listen. There are codes to decipher, all is encrypted in this digital age full of red herrings and blind, closed cul-de-sacs.

Sometimes it takes a mechanical kick-start before inspiration will grace us with its presence. Sometimes the opposite is the case.

It is important to always be aware that we can only affect what we can affect, so at least be sure to do that.

Banish all else that is placed in your way, to bring down your mood, and darken your day; do not allow these sensual intruders to blunt your blades.

The delivery device is your television. It saps your freedom, dumbs down your thoughts to a hum-frequency far below optimal operation. Short periods of rest, without this contraption of interference make this statement crystal clear; the moment you revisit the machine and its efforts to indoctrinate, you are able to feel what true cerebral freedom really is.

We are slaves to all sorts of things, or to nothing, it depends on how we live our lives.

We emerge from the womb understanding all the secrets of life, and it is downhill from there. Work at remembering.

High achievers don't see problems, they solve them. They see a stepping stone to an outcome. They feel every mistake, trip-up and trip-over as feedback, helpful, a lesson on the path to the result, a mere adjustment, en route to their own perception of success - or at least, progress.

It is always very easy to find an excuse why something didn't happen or didn't work, or someone to blame for it.
An achiever looks inward. What must I change to go forward, how do I fix what went wrong? Even in physically reading these words, the reader can only process them according to their ability to understand what the words are saying.

And so to understanding....

In relationships, misunderstandings should be talked fully through, all the way until they have become understandings. It is everybody's fault if it doesn't happen. Over time, if not addressed, the relationship will break, by any of the multiple possible routes.

The word 'narcissist' has become so commonplace, that men may quite believably be hated for just daring to have testosterone in their bodies. Shouting once in a while.

Contrary to myth, we do not find a perfectly compatible partner. Seeking one out is futile. The way that adult devotion and love develop, after a honeymoon period where the 'perfect partner' stage has passed, Is that partners decide to stay together for their whole lives, and each partner's expectation is upon themselves to be the best partner they can be for the other. That is how adults behave in couples. Temptation to stray will come for both, that is a test of maturity. And so forth. It is those who do not appreciate or grasp this, that break the bond, usually through weakness.

In the end, for life-changing things to happen, everyone has to do 'it' on their own.

If I had a penny, for each graduate of the 'University of Life' and 'School of Hard Knocks' that has tried to convince me that formal education has no value, that instincts and beliefs are superior to hard facts and proof, and traditional science teaches nothing, I would have £7462.78.

You don't know when you're going to die.
And by deduction, neither do I.

About the Author

Stuart was born in 1965 in Westminster, London, and brought up in Wiltshire. He studied chemistry at Worcester College, University of Oxford, and went on into financial services where he worked for ten years, reaching an executive-level position at Friends Provident.

In the summer of 1994 that career was cut short by the onset of schizophrenia, with the first of Stuart's psychotic episodes. All in all he was to spend six separate spells in residential care.

Many years later, in 2018, he decided to write seriously. The social and political analysis of his first book 'A United Kingdom' - Trains of Logical Thought was self-published in 2019. Stuart, ambitiously, decided to write the book utilising some experimental syntax and formats, as well as attacking very controversial themes; such as the cultural time-bomb of teenage boys having unfettered access to hard pornography; the right of women to have total autonomy over their bodies; the suggestion that if there were a god she'd be a goddess; a schizophrenic dream sequence; the history of the treatment of tobacco; the actual techniques of propaganda (which are alive and well and very much current) broken down; the illogical ideas of Brexit; studies of the strategies of Margaret Thatcher; of Tony Blair; of David Cameron, of Theresa May. Is it true or not, that the Royal Family "pay for themselves" through tourism as they are always telling us? Or, in fact, has nobody actually addressed whether it's true? Some have suggested the book should be studied in schools and universities.

At this point, summer 2023, Stuart has self-published nine books. Three are full abstract poetry collections, Cosmic Visions (2021), Cataclysmic Vibrations (2022) and Tapestries of Tarot (2023). Two are non-fiction books, 'A United

Kingdom' - Trains of Logical Thought and The Ocean, which tells of the day Stuart and his family scattered his mother's ashes at sea. Four are anthologies featuring international poets - Pandemic Poets contains COVID-related poetry, and the others are a series of books on mental health written by carers, sufferers and survivors, under the title of The Melting Pot Episodes 1, 2 and 3. The fourth collection in the series is being edited now, and it will be the final episode. The mental health charities MIND and SANE have featured the project online.

The other upcoming works are: a second, accompanying book of poetry to Tapestries of Tarot, that is an anthology based on the same theme, poems about individual cards; an autobiographical account of psychosis and actual delusions in the setting of a psychiatric ward - written against a backdrop of Faustian and Satanic themes, from Stuart's harrowing experiences, only made possible by scribbled notes of dreams and hallucinations over almost twenty years.

There is one more collection of Stuart's poetry and prose pieces, to be published, and there is to be a book of classic poetry, contemporary poetry and song lyrics to round things off, the likelihood being that no further projects will be undertaken. Musical collaborations with the rock band Lesoir, from the Netherlands, and Antony Kalugin from the Ukraine, have spread awareness to different sectors and countries.

Stuart lives in Yorkshire, where he has been since moving there in 2012. His catalogue of projects are unique in self-publishing circles, and so far he has not been tempted away by approaches from traditional publishers. One of the essays, in fact, to feature in an upcoming book, blows the lid off traditional publishing operations and 'Creative Writing' qualifications, in the light of AI programs such as ChatGPT (which uses everything those courses contain). Stuart feels that self-publishing, and the related skills, are the future, rather than archaic systems and protocols that drag their heels through "the business"; the result being books that copy the styles of other books and covers that all resemble one another. Writers are frequently signing contracts that give away control over their own intellectual property, in order to access the market. Just like Faust, you could say, or Dorian Gray.

Printed in Great Britain
by Amazon

28057586R00075